G. I. JON

IBO ART

SHIRE ETHNOGRAPHY

2

Cover photograph
Helmet mask, Amobia village, Nri-Awka Ibo, representing a beautiful woman
with hair made up into a solid crested construction to which combs and bells
have been added.

British Library Cataloguing in Publication Data:
Jones, G. I. (Gwilym Iwan).
Ibo art.
— (Shire ethnography; 13).
1. Nigerian sculptures.
I. Title.
730'. 9669.
ISBN 0-7478-0012-X.

Published by
SHIRE PUBLICATIONS LTD
Cromwell House, Church Street, Princes Risborough,
Aylesbury, Bucks HP17 9AJ, UK.

Series Editor: Bryan Cranstone.

ISBN 0 7478 0012 X

First published 1989.

Printed in Great Britain by C. I. Thomas & Sons (Haverfordwest) Ltd,
Press Buildings, Merlins Bridge, Haverfordwest, Dyfed SA61 1XF.

Contents

LIST OF ILLUSTRATIONS 4

1. INTRODUCTION 5

2. DOMESTIC ECONOMY 11

3. MASKS AND MASQUERADES 31

4. CARVED FIGURES AND THEIR USES 37

5. THE NORTHERN IBO AND THEIR NEIGHBOURS 45

6. THE SOUTHERN, CROSS RIVER AND NORTH-EASTERN IBO 49

7. MUSEUMS 68

8. FURTHER READING 70

INDEX 71

4

List of illustrations

1. Map *page 7*
2. Ifogu band, Nkporo tribe *page 9*
3. Carving a figure mask, Rumuji town *page 10*
4. Mba dancer, Nkporo tribe *page 13*
5. Ikem head, Ohuhu Ibo or Anang Ibibio *page 14*
6. Uli designs, Ohuhu-Ngwa Ibo *page 15*
7. Face mask with 'Itchi' marks', Amobia village *page 16*
8. Lughulu mask, Ugwueke Alayi town *page 16*
9. Ugbom figure, Oboro tribe *page 17*
10. Face mask, Nkwelle town *page 18*
11. Obu (meeting house) figures, Asaga town *page 19*
12. Ornamental water pots, Northern Ika Ibo *page 20*
13. Clay figure, Northern Ika Ibo *page 20*
14. House with cement statues, Owerri town *page 21*
15. Ogbukele drum, Ekpeya tribe *page 22*
16. Mbari house, Ulakwo town *page 23*
17. Mbari house, Umowa town *page 23*
18. Mbari house, Southern Oratta Ibo *page 24*
19. Carved door, Nri-Awka Ibo *page 25*
20. Okwa Nzu chalk bowl, Abiriba town *page 27*
21. Hand mirror, Nri-Awka Ibo *page 27*
22. Carved wooden bottles, Awka town *page 28*
23. Ibo stools, Ikwerre and Nri-Awka *page 29*
24. Small boys' masquerade, Abiriba town *page 32*
25. Oji Onu head mask, Nri-Awka Ibo *page 33*
26. Alebo figure mask, Rumuji town *page 33*
27. Twin-figured head-dress, Ogume town *page 34*
28. Janus shoulder mask, Ozu-Item tribe *page 35*
29. Awo Ohia (traveller), Isuochi tribe *page 35*
30. Household shrines, Northern Ika Ibo *page 38*
31. Village tutelary deity, Orsu tribe *page 39*

32. Agu Nsi figure, Nri-Awka Ibo *page 39*
33. Ugbom figure, Olokoro tribe *page 41*
34. Nwamuo dance trophy, Ogume town *page 41*
35. Yam knife, Item tribe *page 42*
36. Ikenga figures, Nimo town *page 42*
37. Ivhri figure, Aboh town *page 43*
38. Ugbom figure, Ibibio *page 43*
39. Mgbedike helmet mask, Nri-Awka Ibo *page 44*
40. Oyibo (white man), Nri-Awka Ibo *page 46*
41. Ajonku skin-covered head, Abiriba town *page 51*
42. Ekpe (Ibo) head, Ngwa Ibo *page 51*
43. Onyejuwe and another female Okorosie mask, Eziama town *page 52*
44. Nwanyure and Akatakpuru Okorosie masks, Eziama town *page 53*
45. Ekeleke masquerade, Orsu tribe *page 54*
46. Ohwa Owu mask, Ekpeya tribe *page 55*
47. Ogbukele head mask of 'were' hippopotamus, Ekpeya tribe *page 55*
48. Abbam Owu figure mask, Rumuji town *page 56*
49. Four female Owu heads, Rumuji town *page 57*
50. Dibia revives Onyechumiri, Akanu town *page 58*
51. Ceremonial drum, Abiriba town *page 60*
52. Ngbangba Ikoro masked band, Abiriba town *page 60*
53. Lughulu comic mask, Item tribe *page 61*
54. Ifogu hooded character, Nkporo tribe *page 62*
55. Ifogu female character, Nkporo tribe *page 62*
56. Initiates in Isiji masquerade, Nkporo tribe *page 63*
57. Mask called Mba, Nkporo tribe *page 64*
58. Ikwumocha Ifogu mask, Nkporo tribe *page 65*
59. Figure of mother and child, Ezza tribe *page 66*
60. Obodo Enyi head mask, Izi tribe *page 67*

1
Introduction

The Ibo (sometimes spelt Igbo), who number between nine or ten million people, are the largest West African group speaking a common language. Linguistic and ethnographic evidence point to their evolution in the Niger valley south of the Anambara River on the savannah forest margin. Here they developed a system of rotational agriculture which enabled them to expand southwards until they reached the Eastern Delta and eastwards as far as the middle Cross River, occupying the whole of the Niger Cross River hinterland apart from its south-eastern corner, which contained the Ibibio people. There was also a lesser movement across the Niger river, which established contact with the Benin kingdom and divided the other Edo-speaking peoples into northern (Ishan and Kukuruku) and southern (Urhobo and Isoko) divisions. The Ibo are now divided by ethnographers into five major groups: Northern, Southern, Western, Eastern or Cross River, and North-eastern. The colonial government grouped the Northern Ibo into the Onitsha province, the Southern Ibo into the Owerri province and the other groups into administrative divisions within the neighbouring provinces. After independence and the Biafran War the Onitsha province, with the addition of the North-eastern Ibo division, has become the Anambara state and the Owerri (less its southern division of Ahoada) the Imo state; the Cross River Ibo were divided between these two states, while the Western Ibo became part of the Bendel state and the Ahoada division part of the Rivers state.

Expansion into the forest was not due to any outside pressures but to increase of population, which was met by a relatively peaceful drift of people from the centre to the periphery. This was followed in what was the original centre by increased economic specialisation and diversification into ritual specialists, blacksmiths, carvers and other craftsmen. These travelled from the centre to live and trade in the surrounding markets, but still kept in touch with their home villages, returning there eventually. This resulted in the development of a very effective system of free trade, operating within an elaborate network of markets and interconnecting trade routes in the Lower Niger area, which came to be dominated in its Ibo part by the 'town' (group of villages) of Nri. This trade network looked northwards towards the middle Niger and the Hausa north. The quantity and quality of the bronze 'treasure' excavated at Igbo Uku, which has been carbon-dated to about AD 700-1020, suggest that it antedated any contact with Europe. Ibo expansion eastwards resulted in similar Ibo specialisations in some of the Cross River Ibo 'towns', notably Abiriba and Arochuku. Their traders and craftsmen travelled northwards towards the Benue and southwards to the Ibibio and the Delta margin beyond, where they traded with the fishing villages.

There was no equivalent political development into large centralised chiefdoms. The whole region remained a mosaic of innumerable, small, autonomous, land-owning, local communities originally referred to as 'towns' and later as village groups, each in a state of rivalry and of armed neutrality or more open hostility with its neighbours. The exception were the North-eastern Ibo, who on moving out of the forest developed into a few large tribes with an organisation more suited to territorial expansion in a savannah environment already inhabited by other people.

With the advent of the overseas slave trade, the fishing villages of Kalabari and Ubani, on the estuary known to the Portuguese as the Rio Real and to later traders as the Bonny River, developed into the trading states of Calabar and Bonny. A century or so later, on the Cross River estuary, the Ibibio villages that called themselves Efik became the trading state which Europeans insisted on calling Old Calabar, distinguishing the original state as New Calabar. These trading states bought their slaves from the 'town' of Arochuku, whose trading organisation (which exploited the reputedly supernatural powers of its tutelary deity) covered most of the hinterland. By now the Northern and Southern Ibo and the Ibibio had become the most densely populated area in West Africa and by 1800 slaves were being shipped from the Bonny River alone at an estimated rate of twenty thousand a year. They were obtained, fortunately, by methods that were far less socially destructive than in other parts of Nigeria: not from slave raiding or as the spoils of intercity warfare (as in the Yoruba west) but by way of trade. The Aros bought any persons their families wished to get rid of, had to part with to meet their debts or who had been kidnapped or betrayed into an ambush. They were immediately removed from their home area and despatched to one or other of the up-river markets of the trading states.

By now most of the original forest had disappeared and been replaced by one of oil palms which could not survive in high forest

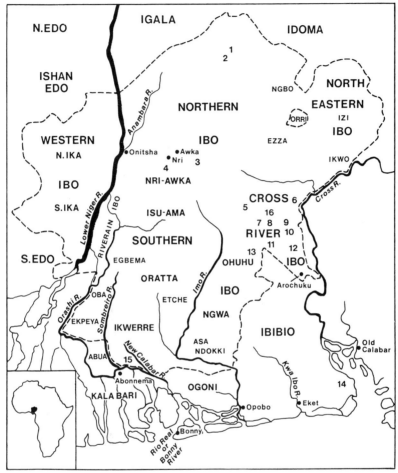

1. Ibo tribal distribution. The broken line denotes the linguistic boundary. Key to tribes and towns represented by numbers: 1 Ibo Omabe; 2 Ibo Odo; 3 Inyi; 4 Igbo Uku; 5 Ugwu Eke Alayi; 6 Afikpo; 7 Item; 8 Abiriba; 9 Ngusu Ada; 10 Asaga Ohaffia; 11 Abam; 12 Akanu Ohaffia; 13 Bende; 14 Oron; 15 Rumuji.

but grew wild around compounds and gardens. In the first quarter of the nineteenth century, when the overseas slave trade was being suppressed, the world needed oil. Most of the Ibo and almost all of the Ibibio country had the trees and the labour to produce the oil as well as the rivers for transporting it in bulk to the ports of Abonnema, Opobo, Eket and Old Calabar. By the end of the century the Oil Rivers Protectorate had been established on the coast, the Royal Niger Company was operating on the Lower Niger and Ibo and Ibibio were trading directly with overseas firms or with their local agents. This early colonial period was probably the Indian summer of Ibo and other East Nigerian art as expressed in their sculpture and domestic crafts. Masks and figures were produced very largely and in considerable quantity by the people in the areas served by these waterways. A few have survived and found their way into museums and private collections, but most have been destroyed in the wave of Christian evangelism that spread over the country in the following century. Every little village wanted its church and the new learning it brought with it. Masks and figures and the cults associated with them were 'juju' (idolatrous); any money that was available for communal purposes now went to the maintenance of the village school and its teacher. Some areas, particularly those with a strong sculptural tradition, survived the change; their masquerades achieved a compromise, the more ancient masks remaining 'juju' and being played by non-Christians, the rest becoming non-'juju' and the concern of Christians. Today, interest in masquerades has revived and they are once more flourishing but they have become secular and lost their former mystery. Some are even played by women. The masks themselves are more vivid and elaborate but, at least to a European eye, have lost much of their former simplicity and refinement.

Styles
    It is customary to divide the sculpture of Eastern Nigeria into four tribal styles: Ibo, Ijo, Ibibio and Ekoi (or Cross River). This, however, is a gross oversimplification. Stylistic boundaries seldom coincide with linguistic or political ones, while the term 'tribe' becomes meaningless when applied to groups as divergent in size as the millions of people speaking Ibo and the few thousand who speak Ekoi. It would be wiser to follow current anthropological usage and reserve the word 'tribe' for smaller groups that share a common name and a belief in a common origin and cultural identity. There are certain obvious features

2. Ifogu masquerade, Nkporo tribe, Cross River Ibo. The band of slit drums and clappers prepares for action, their faces masked with fibre bags. Behind them two Mba dancers relax on chairs.

(for example, the emaciated angular face, the slit eye-holes and the prominent carinated nose) which characterise many of the masks from the Lower Niger area. Since most of those so far collected were carved by Ibos, we can attach this label to them but only if we first realise that there are many other masks carved by Ibos which are not in this style but conform to one of the other three styles or are the independent invention of the carver, and secondly that other people in the Lower Niger area share this so-called Ibo style, namely the Northern and Southern Edo, the Igala and the Idoma.

The social and political climate of Eastern Nigeria favours diversity rather than uniformity. We can distinguish areas with their own local styles, masquerades whose masks and costumes remain the same wherever they may extend and other areas and masquerades where there is variety and change. These complexities are discussed in more detail in the later chapters.

3. Making a figure mask for Owu masquerade with traditional tools of matchet, adze and knives and modern additions of plane, drill and hammer. Rumuji town, Southern Ikwerre Ibo.

2
Domestic economy

Like other Nigerian forest dwellers Ibo men and women were skilled at converting the forest to their own uses, sharing the work between them. Men fought and hunted; women collected. Men cut the forest down and converted it into farm land; women tended and weeded it. Men grew and owned the yams, women all the subsidiary crops. Men climbed the palm trees, using a single climbing rope, and cut the fruit; women processed it into palm oil and sold it in the local markets. Men were the carvers and metal workers, women the potters and the weavers of mats and various kinds of baskets (others were made by men). Women also grew and shaped the gourds and calabashes that provided them with additional basins, bowls, bottles and musical instruments. The wealth provided by the slave trade and later by the palm-oil trade enabled them to acquire and make their own additional imports, notably cotton cloth, guns and gunpowder, and thus expand their domestic economy and add to its resources, though this also led to the disappearance of some of their artefacts and local industries.

Tools and weapons

Ibo weapons originally consisted of a matchet (cutlass), throwing spears and daggers of various sizes. Their domestic equipment was again a matchet, a light short-handled iron-bladed hoe and various axes, adzes, chisels and knives, some of the latter the special property of women. Trees were felled with matchets until the introduction of cross-cut saws at the end of the nineteenth century. Spears have long since disappeared and been replaced by muzzle-loading muskets known to the trade as 'Dane guns'. Apart from a few iron-shafted ceremonial spears attached to the shrines of various spirits, none has been collected. Fighting matchets were of two types. In the Lower Niger area they consisted of a curved, single-edged sword about 18 inches (45 cm) long and in the Cross River area of a short, straight, two-edged heavy-headed knife. Both types are shown on figures carved in these two areas but have been replaced by imported wrought iron matchets used for farm work (figure 3) and by 16 inch (41 cm) steel hunting knives used for more lethal purposes. Local blacksmiths continue to make the hoes and other iron tools.

Weaving and dress
The Lower Niger is where the cotton weaving of the Western and Central Sudan ends and the raffia weaving of the Cameroons and Congo forests takes over. Cotton is grown and woven on the western side of the Lower Niger among the Edo and Western Ibo, who make short lengths of plain white or striped yellow and blue cloth; the Igala and a few Northern Ibo towns weave lengths of blue cloth striped in red, yellow and other colours; the Ngbo tribe of Northern Ibo, like their Idoma neighbours, produce short blue and white towels which they wear around their waists; and far south on the Lower Imo the Ndokki villages weave superior false embroidered cloths called Akwete, worn as skirts by those who can afford them and woven out of imported cotton yarn. They had the same patterns as those used by the Yoruba town of Ijebu Ode in the Lagos area, which in the days of the slave trade was noted for its export of cotton cloths.

There is no word for indigo in the Ibo language. The Northern Ibo preferred dark red from powdered camwood, which they rubbed on to their bodies and into the white cotton clothes which they wore as cloaks. The Yoruba type of indigo dyeing has only recently spread to the Ibo area and to the town of Ezillu (Northern Ibo), where imported white baft is resist-dyed in local patterns and sold under the name of Ukara cloth.

Men and women were originally unclothed except for a loincloth. On ceremonial occasions they relied on cloths imported from other parts of Nigeria and increasingly from overseas, including superior hats, coats, army uniforms and other fine second-hand clothing. These became the 'traditional African dress' for colonial state occasions and were depicted on figures of ancestors and other carvings, particularly the top hat, which during the nineteenth century replaced all other imported headgear. Another Victorian import was the dress shirt: this became the prototype for the 'Opobo gown' (figure 14), which is now the standard ceremonial wear for the Ibo gentlemen. It was originally worn over a skirt, consisting of two yards of imported 'Real India' or Akwete cloth reaching from the waist to the ankles.

In most Ibo villages they still weave raffia into strips that can be sewn into bags and sacks and use it and other fibres to make coil and woven baskets of various shapes and sizes; pliable sleeping mats are made from the fibre of the screw pine. The Southern Ibo and Ibibio use a rectangular carrying basket with a wooden bottom and low basketwork sides. Among the Northern Ibo this

4. Ifogu masquerade, Nkporo tribe, Cross River Ibo. The Mba dancer wears a black felt hat, scarlet singlet and cotton print skirt tied up in front to give freedom of action. An ivory bracelet is on his right arm, one of white goatskin on his left, and he carries a magic rattle.

type of basket is restricted to men, women preferring flat circular ones supported on a separate wooden disc. These have been replaced today very largely by imported enamel basins.

Personal adornment

As befitted a people wearing a minimum of clothing, Ibo had many ways of decorating their heads and bodies. Women concentrated on their hair and on painting decorative patterns on

5. Ikem masquerade, Ohuhu Ibo or Anang Ibibio. Female head with the hair dressed into five curved 'horns'. This is a modern carving painted in oils and varnished; in older carvings the face and neck were covered in skin. (Pitt Rivers Museum, Oxford. Drawing by Dr K. F. Campbell.)

their bodies, men on scarring their faces and, among the North-eastern Ibo, the torsos of their women. Most of these skills are no longer practised and survive only on Ibo masks and figures, providing us with clues on where they were made and used.

Hairdressing

Women kept the hair of their young children short and used a razor to shave curvilinear patterns in it. (Barbers today cut the hair of younger men in various European styles, using a razor to emphasise the partings.) Old men and women found it convenient to keep their heads shaved. Younger women usually kept their hair close to their head in short, tight plaits or tied up into little bunches. On more special occasions (for example, before marriage or after the birth of their first baby), they trained it out and tied it into long, curved 'horns' or, particularly amongst the Northern Ibo, moulded it with clay, charcoal and oil into solid structures decorated with combs, pins, ribbons, bells and other

6. Uli designs, Ohuhu-Ngwa Ibo. Normally painted on people's bodies, these were reproduced on paper by women in the Bende divisional prison.

ornaments. Both forms indicated, among other things, that the wearer's relatives were wealthy enough to free her temporarily from any heavy manual labour as, until the headdress had been cut or shaved off, she was unable to carry any loads on her head. Both styles were copied and exaggerated in Ibo sculpture, the 'horned' version on heads carved in the Cross River style (figure 5), the solid crests on the helmet masks of the Nri-Awka Ibo (cover photograph).

Body painting

Women used various chalks, yellow and red earths or powdered woods to paint overall patterns on the exposed portions of

7. (Left) Face mask, Amobia village, Nri-Awka Ibo, showing 'Itchi' scarring on forehead. Part of the insignia of the Nze members of the Ozio title society.
8. (Right) Lughulu masquerade, Ugwueke Alayi town, Isu-Item Ibo. Mask representing a beautiful female spirit.

their own and their menfolk's bodies (figure 20). A more sophisticated art, which has now died out, was that of Uli painting. This used a stain made from the Uli creeper to paint curvilinear designs which showed up black on a dark skin and blue on a white one (figure 6); this illustration gives some idea of the overall design but not of how it looks on a rounded human body.

Facial marks

A more permanent method of pattern-making was to carve them in human skin in such a way that the flesh, as it healed, formed into raised lumps called keloids or into long gashes, either raised or depressed. Though often referred to as 'tribal marks', these were primarily intended as marks of beauty or in some cases of social rank. Most have long ceased to be made and survive only on masks and figures.

9. Ugbom figure, Oboro tribe, Ohuhu Ibo, carried in the Ugbom trophy dance. The basketry cap into which it fits should rest on the bearer's head.

First in this category were the 'Itchi marks' of the Northern Ibo, indicative of membership of the Ozo title society, which extended over most of the Northern Ibo and to the Isuama group of Southern Ibo (figure 7). These marks consisted of diagonal gashes across the entire forehead and upper eyelids. They seem to have a very ancient ancestry for very similar marks were depicted on the foreheads of the heads and figures of the Igbo Uku treasure.

The Central Ijo had a raised vertical scar down the centre of their foreheads, a mark which they shared with the neighbouring Western Ibo. This scar is also found on Ibibio masks and on those of the Isu-Item Ibo (figure 8). The Southern Edo and their Western Ibo neighbours were distinguished by a series of four to six broad vertical depressed gashes on their foreheads, a form of scarring peculiar to this part of the Delta margin (figures 30 and 37).

Many Yoruba groups favoured short vertical or horizontal

10. Face mask, Nkwelle town, Nri-Awka Ibo, with representation of facial paintings on forehead and cheeks.

gashes on their cheeks. This fashion is not found east of the Lower Niger, the Ibo and Cross River people preferring instead diagonals, usually a single-edged or double-edged line from below the eye to the corner of the jaw; these are found on masks and heads of the Ohuhu-Ngwa and Cross River Ibo carved in both the Ibo and the Cross River styles (figures 41, 42). Keloids were cut on the temples and between the eyebrows, either two or three together or in vertical rows. These were used by the Idoma and also by the Ohuhu-Ngwa Ibo and Ibibio (figures 9, 33 and 42).

Representations of these facial scars can easily be confused with the circles, crosses and other simple figures that were painted on people and reproduced on their carvings. The most striking of these are the curved triangles stretched diagonally across the cheeks and foreheads of many of the Nri-Awka Ibo white-faced masks (figure 10).

Beadwork and jewellery

Beadwork is conspicuous by its absence in the Ibo country and in other parts of Eastern Nigeria. People rely today on imported jewellery. Traces of beadwork were found with the Igbo Uku treasure, and beads of all sorts and in considerable quantity were imported through the Rio Real in the days of the slave trade, but they had all disappeared by the nineteenth century except for a few very ancient 'Cambay' beads (single large agate beads said to come from India) and leopards' canine teeth. The latter are worn at the throats of elderly people and are represented on Ibo figures and other carvings (figure 31).

Ivory carving

Nri-Awka Ibo carvers were said to work in ivory, though none of their work has been collected. Ibo ivory work seems to have been confined to simple undecorated tusk horns and, in the Nri-Awka area, to solid and heavy armlets and even larger and heavier anklets (figure 11). These are treasured heirlooms and worn only on festive occasions. The ivory tusk horns are no

11. Obu figures, Asaga town, Ohaffia tribe, Cross River Ibo, placed in the village meeting house (Obu) and made in honour of its founder and tutelary deity. Said to represent spirit members of his household: a man drinking wine through a straw, his new wife before her marriage (hence heavy anklets of brass rods wound around and above her ankles), a masquerader in the costume of an 'Egbo runner' and a rich woman with ivory anklets, her hair built up into a solid crest so that she has to carry her basket on her shoulder.

different from those in other parts of the region; a few have crude, simple designs engraved on them.

Pottery

Pottery was an exclusively female craft dispersed over most of the Ibo country wherever there was suitable clay and a local demand for it. There were, however, two important centres whose superior wares had a wider distribution, Inyi in the Nri-Awka area and Ishiago on the Eastern Railway and connected by road to the Cross River. Pots were made predominantly by the coil method and their quality and range of forms were much the same as in other parts of Nigeria. They were mainly water and other pots, bowls and platters, and they were either left plain, burnished, decorated with incised lines and circles or given an overall indented pattern with rollers. Some, however, were made for display in spirit shrines or meeting houses; these were modelled with raised curvilinear bands, bosses and ornamental handles.

Some potters liked to add little human figures below the rim of their pots; a few made separate, crude figures like the one illustrated in figure 13. A further development was made by a potter in the Western Ibo town of Ossisa who modelled

12. Ornamental water pots, Northern Ika Ibo, drying in the sun before firing.

13. Clay figure of mother and child, Northern Ika Ibo.

14. Modern house, Owerri town, Oratta Ibo, with cement statues of its owner, a motor transport magnate, and symbols of his (horse)power.

remarkably fine naturalistic figures. Some of her work was brought to England in 1880 and found its way to the Museum of Mankind in London. The rest has disappeared. A speciality of the Northern Ibo was a water pot with a circular hole in the side which, when struck with the palm of the hand, gave out a resonant note. It was used as one of the musical instruments in the bands that accompanied their masquerades.

Most superior native pottery has now disappeared and been replaced by imported European glazed earthenware jugs and plates (the last often being inset by the Southern Ibo into the walls of their houses).

Mud sculpture

Ibo women rubbed a fine clay into the mud benches, pedestals and walls of their houses to give them a polished finish. They occasionally inset into them bright stones, glazed earthenware and similar decorations. More rarely they painted their walls or

15. Ogbukele Society drum, Ekpeya tribe, Riverain Ibo. Note the trophy of skulls of leopards killed by members of the society.

made drawings on them. Ibo men who lived near the Ibibio hired their fresco painters to decorate walls.

Medicine men and priests made the conical anthropomorphic mud shrines called Ibudu and men and women with a gift for it often modelled ancestral and other human figures on the verandahs of their houses. Mud sculpture has largely been displaced today by modelling in cement, which usually takes the form of life-size painted statues of the living or recently deceased and seeks to be as realistic as possible (figure 14).

Musical instruments

No definitive study has yet been made of Ibo musical instruments and Ibo music. Today the music takes two forms.

16. (Left) Mbari house, Ulakwo town, Oratta Ibo, in honour of Ale, its tutelary deity, shown seated holding an ivory horn and with one of her children at her knee.

17. (Right) Mbari house, Umowa town, Oratta Ibo, just completed, 1933.

That which is found in the bars and night-clubs of Nigerian cities looks overseas for its inspiration. The other, which still accompanies masquerades and other playing and dancing, relies predominantly on singing and drumming; the instruments are mainly slit drums (sometimes called gongs) of all sort and sizes, true (or membrane) drums, clappers, xylophones, metal gongs, pots, horns, whistles and rattles (some made of beaded calabashes, others of small baskets or gourds filled with seeds). Instruments played on their own are sanzas with calabash resonators and the elephant tusk horns that form the insignia of chiefs and important people. Stringed instruments are uncommon apart from those acquired in other parts of Nigeria.

Housing

Ibo housing was conditioned primarily by the rainfall, which is heavier in the south and diminishes northwards. Thus the Southern and the Cross River Ibo built rectangular houses with

18. Mbari house, Southern Oratta Ibo, in honour of Ale, its tutelary deity, shown feasting with two attendants, one holding a horn. Beyond are figures of a woman, a white cat, an ostrich and a policeman.

walls of mud supported by a stick framework and roofed with tile-like mats made from the leaves of the raffia palm, which also supplied the rafters and purlins. Northern Ibo had rectangular houses with solid mud walls and the same raffia-mat roofs. North-eastern Ibo houses were of solid mud but square with a conical grass-thatched roof. Western Ibo in the south had the same rectangular houses with lath and plaster walls as their Southern Edo neighbours. In the north they followed the Yoruba pattern of a large, solid-walled, many-roomed square house built around a central courtyard. Except for this last type Ibo houses were arranged in compounds that were fenced in the south, walled in the north.

The Cross River Ibo and the Ekpeya tribe of Southern Ibo built superior meeting houses for their secret societies, many of which were elaborately decorated, some with figures of men and women and of Ekpe (Egbo) masqueraders (figure 11). Today those who can afford it have replaced these houses built out of local materials with permanent structures with cement-block walls and corrugated iron roofs.

Mbari houses

Oratta and Etche Ibo villages built houses which they called Mbari in honour of their tutelary deities. These consisted of a highly conventionalised model of a two-storeyed house with the house itself shrunk to a single room and surrounded by a greatly enlarged verandah. On this was displayed a larger-than-life figure of the deity seated with his or her spouse and children and surrounded by a great number of smaller figures taken from mythology, local history and contemporary life, some arranged singly, others grouped together in tableaux (figures 16-18).

Metalwork

Iron was smelted in the north of the region wherever there were lateritic outcrops and particularly along the ridge of high

19. Carved wooden door, Nri-Awka Ibo, forming gateway into walled compound.

ground running south from Udi to Okigwi and then east to Ohaffia. The original currency was of iron, which still survived in the early colonial days as small, conventionalised arrowheads in the Abaja area (Northern Ibo) and in the larger three-pointed star-shaped pieces of the North-eastern Ibo. However, this original coinage had long been replaced by the cowrie currency of the Lower Niger area and the trade currencies of manillas (metal bracelets) among the Southern Ibo and Ibibio and the brass rods of the Cross River. Locally smelted iron had also been displaced by imported iron bars. Ironworking was an important Ibo industry, in which many of their towns specialised. Their travelling blacksmiths covered the whole of the Eastern Region and also extended to the western side of the Lower Niger. The most famous were from the towns of Awka (Northern Ibo), Nwkerre (Southern Ibo) and Item and Abiriba (Cross River Ibo), while smiths from the Ezza tribe made the very large, circular hoes of the North-eastern Ibo. Apart from a few ceremonial iron-shafted spears and the iron-belled staffs used by priests of various cults, blacksmiths' work was confined to utilitarian objects, though some specialised as gunsmiths repairing muzzle-loading flintlock muskets and converting them into 'cap guns'.

Compared with the Yoruba cities or Benin, there was little interest in working in semi-precious metals. Local smiths made brass, silver or other white-metal combs, pins, brass gongs and small ornamental bells and on occasion more substantial objects, but there was little or no demand for such work and the petty chiefs on either side of the Lower Niger preferred to obtain their brass regalia from Benin. The superb bronze work of the Igbo Uku treasure was a unique and long-forgotten occurrence.

Woodcarving

Ibo were skilled woodcarvers, particularly those of the town of Awka and other towns in the Nri-Awka group. With their simple tools they were able to cut down iroko and other large hardwood trees and, with the aid of wedges, fire and boiling water, convert them into the canoes which seventeenth-century travellers described as 'the largest in the Ethiopias of Guinea', into their great Ikoro war drums, carved out of the trunks of iroko trees, or the solid doors that closed the entrances to their walled compounds (figure 19). Smaller pieces of wood were made into troughs and mortars, slit and membrane drums (figure 51), bowls and dishes of various shapes and sizes, stools and headrests, clubs and staffs and handles of all sorts. The introduction of cross-

20. Okwa Nzu chalk bowl, Abiriba town, Cross River Ibo, in which chalk is offered to visiting strangers. Note the dark Uli designs on the holder's stomach and hand and her overall body painting in yellow ochre.

21. Hand mirror, Nri-Awka Ibo. The front is inset with a small piece of mirror glass. (Cambridge University Museum of Archaeology and Anthropology. Drawing by Dr K. F. Campbell.)

cutting and other saws in the late nineteenth century simplified tree-felling and provided the Ibo with planks and deckings to panel the walls of their meeting houses and to increase their range of boxes, chests, benches and lightweight chairs and stools.

Most of these objects were purely functional and left plain and undecorated. Some, however, were intended as works of art and valued as such by their proud owners, as were the masks and other objects carved out of softer wood for their masquerades and for the embellishment of their shrines and meeting houses. Doors, panels and other smooth surfaces were decorated with incised patterns of diagonal and cross-hatched lines, concentric circles and other simple geometric forms in a style used extensively by the Nri-Awka Ibo but found in less developed forms throughout the Ibo country. The style was similar to that

22. Wooden bottles, Awka town, Nri-Awka Ibo. Carved in the form of earthenware palm wine jars.

found higher up the Niger but the designs were different: Nupe and Yoruba using interlaced and endless knots and four- and eight-pointed stars, Ibos pointed triangles and the four-leafed clover (cassava leaf in local parlance).

Most of the utensils were common to West Africa; a few were peculiar to particular Ibo areas. Among these were the chalk bowls of the Abiriba and neighbouring Cross River Ibo. These held a piece of chalk and were presented by a family head to a visiting stranger, who marked his wrist with it to indicate that he was under the protection of the offerer (figure 20). Another was a type of dish with a lidded central portion and a small, circular platform to cut meat on. This was made and used mainly among the Northern and North-eastern Ibo for offering a ceremonial meal (a small piece of meat) to a visitor. A third speciality were the hand mirrors of the Northern and Southern Ibo, which were carved either in the geometric Ibo style or in more curvilinear patterns (figure 21).

To prove their expertise, the Ibo also occasionally carved wooden bottles in imitation of local earthenware ones (figure 22).

Stools. In the past all married Ibo women used carved stools small enough to be carried in their market baskets (figure 23c). Senior men also had large, more impressive stools that were

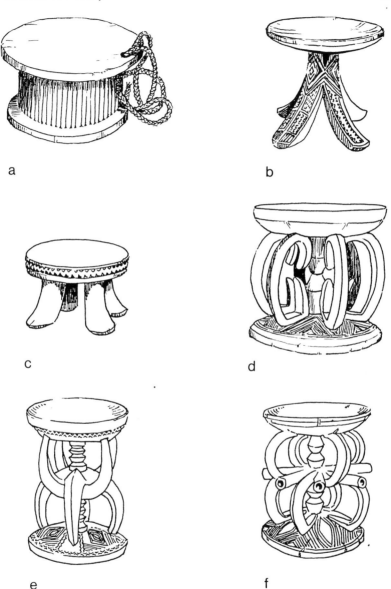

23. Ibo stools, Ikwerre and Nri-Awka. (a) Ikwerre Ibo box stool; (b) Awka pedestal stool carved in Awka town; (c) small stool used by market women; (d,e,f) other types of stool made by Nri-Awka carvers for titled men. (Cambridge University Museum of Archaeology and Anthropology. Drawing by Dr K. F. Campbell.)

carried for them to sit on at village meetings. Today most of these have disappeared and been replaced by upright and folding chairs and, in the case of the market stools, by even lighter ones made by local carpenters. Ibo stools were typically circular, made out of a cylindrical section of tree trunk with most of the centre cut away to lighten it, and leaving an upper and lower disc, the former being hollowed to fit the seat of the user. The Ekpeya and other Riverain Ibo also made lighter stools from a broad ring of bark, the edges of which were sewn on to an upper and lower wooden disc (figure 23a).

The Edo and Ibo on the western side of the Niger carved square or rectangular stools, some like crude Ashanti stools, others more bench-like, as also did the Ibibio, to judge by their carved figures, for no Ibibio stools have survived or been collected. Higher up the Niger two kinds of stool were carved, one with a square seat supported on four legs, one at each corner, the other with a circular seat supported on eight to ten tubular legs. These were locally referred to as Nupe stools to distinguish them from the Ibo stools sold in the same riverain markets, which were carved by Awka and other Nri-Awka carvers. A further distinguishing feature between them was that Nupe carvers incised geometric patterns on the seats of their stools, while Awka carvers polished the seats and incised their designs on the underside. In the early part of the twentieth century there was a small but flourishing industry in Awka making superior stools in which the central portion consisted of various arrangements of narrow, curved supports. Some of these were said to define membership of the various grades in the Ozo title society (figure 23 d-f). A special Awka type of stool (figure 23 b) consisted of a saucer-like seat supported on a central pedestal ending in four splayed feet. (The number four is of ritual significance in Ibo cosmology.)

3
Masks and masquerades

Masquerades, ceremonial performances in which actors impersonating supernatural beings were paraded and displayed to the
public, were an exclusively male domain from which women and
children were strictly excluded, though uninitiated small boys
were encouraged to 'play at masquerading' (figure 24). The word
'mask' is often applied to these entities but here they will be
referred to as 'characters', reserving 'mask' for that part of the
costume representing the head. Even so, 'mask' has to compre-
hend a great variety of headgear, ranging from faceless characters, where the actor's own face is covered by a bag of cotton
cloth or raffia netting, to great pyramids of interlocking human
and animal figures. It can also be made of all sorts of materials:
cloth, raffia, leather or various plastics, but predominantly wood,
normally softwood.

Masks
Masks can be divided into four categories.
True masks. Representations of a human or animal face, worn
either vertically over the actor's face, when it can be called a face
mask, or, if representing a water spirit, antelope or goat,
horizontally on top of the actor's head, when it can be called a
head mask (figure 25).
Heads. Representations of a human or animal head with or
without a neck (figure 49).
Headdresses. Representations of hats, caps, hair arrangements,
animal horns and other more elaborate superstructures (figure
54).
Figures. Complete human or animal figures, the former held
vertically, the latter horizontally (figures 26 and 27).
All except the face masks are worn on top of the actor's head
or, if they are very large, hollowed out to fit over it and to rest on
his shoulders. Figures and heads may be fitted into a basketry cap
which can be attached more firmly to the actor's head and to the
costume.
Masks can be given one or more faces; they can combine
human and animal features; they can be joined to a headdress
and carved from a single piece of wood to form a helmet mask
(cover); a head can be given two faces and become a Janus mask,
or three or four and, if large enough to rest on the actor's

shoulders, become a shoulder mask (figure 28). A neck can end in two or four heads joined together at the back or expand into a bar and carry two separate heads. Figures, whether animal or human, can be carried separately, combined together in tableaux or built up into superstructures of the Ekwe or Nwamuo type (figure 34). They can also, when reduced in size, be added to masks and headdresses as additional decorations. The variations and combinations are considerable, as is the range of styles in which they are carved, and when Ibo artists run out of ideas they have no difficulty in borrowing from elsewhere. Ibo masks with pathological features or with a ring around their forehead have copied Ibibio models; those with a movable lower jaw may have

24. Small boys' masquerade, Abiriba town, Cross River Ibo. They are using an old discarded mask.

25. (Left) Mau masquerade, Nri-Awka Ibo. Mask for a character called Oji Onu (long mouth) or Ulaga, representing a foolish antelope spirit.

26. (Right) Owu masquerade, Rumuji town, Southern Ikwerre Ibo. Figure mask called Alebo representing Tortoise, the trickster character of Ibo folk tales.

copied Ogoni ones (figure 46).

Masquerades

A masquerade can be limited to the parade of one or two characters who are believed to be spirits from the surrounding waste land or water, brought by members of the society that ministers to them to visit the village and then returned there. Most societies, particularly today, increase the number of these characters and support them with a drumming band and an unmasked singing and dancing chorus. The characters appear separately and mime or dance, usually on their own or in pairs; only rarely, and in those areas bordering the Ibibio, have masquerades developed into a dramatic performance in which all the characters combine together in a play, normally a comedy or farce.

The characters in these masquerades are said to be spirits and in the older and simpler ones they can be divided into two main

27. Ogonya masquerade, Ogume town, Southern Ika Ibo. Twin-figure headdress.

types: beautiful, serene, normally feminine characters, and horrific, fierce and masculine ones. Ibo colour symbolism makes the 'beautiful' ones white and the 'fierce' ones black or red and, to increase their fierceness, aggressive animal features like horns and tusks are added. When additional characters are introduced they are taken from mythology (for example, Tortoise, the Ibo 'Brer Rabbit', figure 26), from everyday life (for example, simple, comic or old men or women who, though respected in real life, are guyed in masquerades) or from the natural world around them (for example, wild or domestic animals, fishes or birds).

The generic name for these characters and their masquerades among the Northern Ibo and Ibibio was 'ghost': Mo or Mau in Ibo, Ekpo in Ibibio. In the Delta they were thought of as water spirits, Owu. On the Cross River they were said to be spirits of the forest or waste land and had no common name. Their most widely distributed society and masquerade were called Ekpe, which the Efik of Old Calabar took over from their Ekoi neighbours and developed into a graded wealth society whose higher grades were restricted to those who could afford the exorbitant entrance fees. This Ekpe, known to European traders as Egbo, was distributed up the Cross River as far as Mamfe in the Cameroons. Ekpe was a spirit character that was never seen but only heard and the characters in Ekpe masquerades were said to be his attendant spirits. Ekpe is the Ibibio and Efik word for 'leopard' but this society should not be confused with the so-called Human Leopard Societies, whose members were believed to transform themselves into leopards and in this form to kill their enemies.

28. Ozu-Item tribe, Isu-Item Ibo Janus shoulder mask, Ikem masquerade. Covered in skin with hair represented by circular studs and four wooden horns, with porcupine quills between them and in the mouth of one of the faces. (Drawing by Dr K. F. Campbell.)

29. Mau masquerade, Isuochi tribe, Northern Ibo. Character called Awo Ohia (Traveller) in 'Egbo runner' net costume of Cross River Ekpe (Egbo) masquerades.

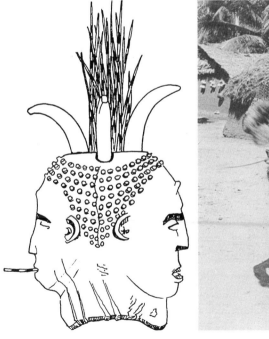

Societies

The organisations responsible for producing these masquerades are often referred to as secret societies. Certainly most of their activities were private and were not revealed to non-members, but this was also true for the business of most associations in Eastern Nigeria, some of which produced masquerades while some did not. The term is more suitably reserved for associations like the Ekpe society described above, which governed the town in the name of this forest spirit who was heard but never seen. The organisers of these masquerades, the actors and other performers were the young men of the village with an interest in masquerading and with the leisure to indulge in it, though older men with a liking and a gift for it were not debarred from continuing to participate. In villages like those of the Northern Edo or the Ada group of Cross River Ibo which were run by their age organisations, masquerading was one of the functions of a particular junior age grade and formed part of the passage rituals of each age set as it moved from the grade of 'boys' into the grade of 'junior men'. In Old Calabar and in the Ibo villages which have adopted the Ekpe society it was the young men of the lower grades of Ekpe who produced the masquerades and who, disguised in the tight-fitting net costumes of 'Egbo runners' (figure 29), carried out the orders of the executive grade of 'Brass Egbo'. Among the Northern and Isu Ibo the Ozo, another graded wealth society, was the power behind the village council but it had no association with any supernatural beings. Masquerading was the concern of younger men organised in each ward into societies specifically concerned with the maintenance of one or two masked characters. These younger men were available to perform their own masquerade or to join with characters from the other wards in a more comprehensive performance.

4
Carved figures and their uses

Ibo use wooden figures of varying sizes for a number of different purposes. We have already referred in the previous chapter to those used in masquerades, which we can distinguish as 'animated' inasmuch as they were held to be alive and active, and in the case of the aggressive ones were prevented from attacking the onlookers only by the intervention of their attendants, who held them in check with ropes or chains around the actor's waist. The figures we are now describing were thought of as inanimate objects, not as living beings. Even when they represented a tutelary or other spirit they were held to be purely a representation of this spirit and a means of communicating with it. They could possess, like any other part of the spirit's shrine, some of its supernatural power but they were never considered as a living being, distinct from the spirit they represented. Such figures can be divided into the following broad categories.

Cult figures

Cult figures were representations of various kinds of spirits, some of which were communal, belonging to the whole town or village, while others were personal, belonging to a single individual. In the first group were representations of tutelary nature spirits, the guardians of a particular locality and associated with a river, hill or other topographical feature and with the community living there. Chuku, the Ibo High God, and Ale (or Ane), the female deity of the land, were never represented in this way (except in some Oratta Mbari houses, but in these cases it was a local emanation of Ale who was the tutelary spirit of the village that made the Mbari — see figure 16). Nor were figures used in ancestor cults except for a few anthropomorphic Ofo (wooden symbol of ancestral authority) and among the Western Ibo, where human figures attached to some of their household shrines were said to represent the founder of a family (figure 30). Diviners might also occasionally advise a widow or close relative to erect a figure of the deceased on his grave. Cult figures of tutelary deities were made principally among the Northern and Isuama Ibo (figure 31). Among the Nri-Awka and Western Isuama they were kept in the priest's house and were produced and displayed by the shrine on special occasions. Among the Eastern Isuama and neighbouring Oratta villages large figures representing the deity and his or her spouse and children were attached to the shrine and occasionally had a roof built over them. The Abam and some other Cross River Ibo carved single figures of local deities which they erected on or beside the principal shrine and in the same area Abiriba and some Ohaffia towns decorated their meeting houses with figures of men and women, 'Egbo runners' and other characters which were said to represent the spirit servants of the tutelary deity in whose honour the house was made.

Quite as important, particularly in the Lower Niger area, were the figures representing personal deities decorating the meeting houses of wealthy Northern Ibo men, who vied with each other in such displays. The best known of these cults was the Ikenga (see below). Northern and Southern Ibo diviners carried with them as part of their paraphernalia their Agu Nsi, small carvings of humans, animals, Ikenga and other ritual objects which were believed to help them in their divination (figure 32).

30. Household shrines, Northern Ika Ibo. They include an ancestral figure, an Ikenga, symbols of lesser cults, medicines and a farming cutlass.

31. (Left) Village tutelary deity, Orsu tribe, Isuama Ibo, standing in front of her shrine with her two Ikenga and a water pot used in rituals associated with her. Note her necklace of leopards' teeth.

32. (Right) Diviner's Agu Nsi, Nri-Awka Ibo, representing a familiar spirit who aids him in his work.

Dance emblems

One of the many kinds of Ibo dances consisted of men or women dancing in a ring around an emblem or trophy which was displayed either standing on its own or borne aloft on a bearer's head. For example, in Cross River war dances the emblem was a horizontal rectangular frame covered in leopard skin to which human skulls or wooden imitations of them were attached, together with rams' skulls and other ornaments. In some (often labelled fertility) dances the emblem was a single human figure, as in the Ugbom dance of the Ohuhu-Ngwa Ibo (figures 9 and 33), or a construction of many figures, as in the Nwamuo dances of the Western Ibo (figure 34).

Toys and ornaments

These were carved as dolls for small children or as small ornaments for attachment to masks and headdresses.

Decorative figures

The ends of Ikoro war drums and other smaller drums were carved into a single head or a seated figure. Membrane drums were often supported on the heads of three caryatid figures (figure 51). Human and animal figures were often carved in bas-relief on the side of drums (figure 15), on doors or on other flat surfaces, and the handles of knives and bowls were often carved in human form (figure 35).

While, as already mentioned, some of these carvings, particularly the cult figures, were felt to be imbued with mystical power or as providing a means of communication with the spirit, others were valued for more secular reasons. In the case of some of the trophy dances, for instance, there was no consensus of opinion: some people considered the figures 'juju': others felt that the 'power' (for example, of promoting fertility, bringing good fortune and so on) lay in the dance itself, or that failure to perform it might bring misfortune to the village.

Ikenga figures

The best known Ibo personal cult and the one that has given rise to the greatest number of carvings is that of Ikenga, a Lower Niger cult of a man's right arm and of success associated with it, which the Edo shared with the Western, Northern, most of the Southern Ibo and with Igala groups. The Ohuhu-Ngwa, Cross River and North-eastern Ibo did not participate in it. Most Ibo and Edo had a small cylindrical object with some geometrical carving on it and ending in a pair of pointed horns. Some Western Ibo increased the size so that it looked more like a circular stool. Other Ibo and Edo added a head and some carved a whole figure. The Nri-Awka Ibo produced the most elaborate cult objects and in the greatest number. Older examples carved by them elaborated the horns and the head, which was shown smoking a pipe. Later ones consisted of complete figures which were shown standing or more usually seated on a circular stool with a cutlass in one hand and a human head in the other (figure 36) or, alternatively, holding a tusk horn and an ornamental staff.

Ivhri

Another personal cult of more limited range was the Ivhri of

33. (Left) Ugbom figure, Olokoro tribe, Ohuhu Ibo, used in Ugbom trophy dance which was originally borrowed from neighbouring Anang Ibibio. Arms of Ibibio figures are often nailed or pegged on. This Ibo figure may have copied one that had lost its arms.
34. (Right) Nwamuo dance, Ogume town, Southern Ika Ibo. The trophy consists of two or more tiers of pairs of male and female figures, two pairs in each tier. It is often surmounted by a pair of birds.

the Southern Edo and adjacent Western Ibo. This cult was concerned with the control of a man's aggressive instincts and was represented by a human figure or figures standing or seated on the back of a conventionalised hippopotamus (figure 37).

Ugbom (Ogbom)

The Ohuhu-Ngwa Ibo had a trophy dance in which women

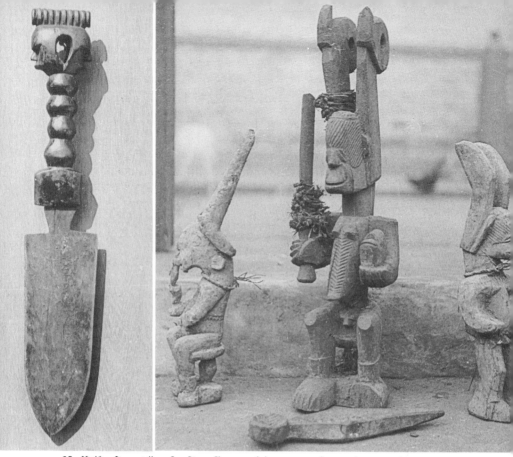

35. Knife, Item tribe, Isu-Item Ibo, used by women for cutting up yams.

36. Ikenga figures, Nimo town, Nri-Awka Ibo. The one in the centre has a cutlass and a human head; the one on the left is drinking palm wine through a straw.

danced around a figure which was carried on a man's shoulders or head and decorated with ribbons and coloured streamers; these were tied to a revolving wheel attached to a rod which passed through a hole in the base of the statue. They called the figure Ugbom and said that they had obtained it from the Ibibio. Most of the figures were collected in the 1930s, when the play had long been discontinued. All that could be learned about it was that it was danced to bring good luck and to promote fertility. The Ugbom was a single male or female figure, mainly the latter (figure 9). Some were shown standing, others seated on rectangular Ibibio-style stools. Most were carved with arms: in some these were pegged or nailed on (an Ibibio feature), while others were carved without any arms (figure 33). They were carved in a number of different styles. Some had birds and other figures added and others were reduced to an abstract form consisting of an upright piece of wood shaped like a half moon with heads both at the top and at the bottom, one looking forward, the other back. Memory of this dance had faded in the Ibibio country by 1937 when K. C. Murray made his survey nor had any Ugbom figures survived. However, there remain in European collections about six male figures (figure 38) and two similar to the half moon type (but lacking the second head). They resembled each other so closely that they could have been carved by the same man but no details of their provenance have been preserved. The four in the

37. (Left) Ivhri figure, Aboh town, Riverain Ibo. The two figures are standing on the representation of a hippopotamus. (Pitt Rivers Museum, Oxford.)

38. (Right) Ugbom figure, provenance unknown, Ibibio. (From the Wellcome Museum, now in the Museum of Mankind, London. Drawing by Dr K. F. Campbell.)

Agar Collection were said to come from Eket and this name was given to the others when they appeared in the auction rooms. This is not very helpful as this name is applied to the port of the Kwa Ibo river, to a small Ibibio tribe related to the Oron and to an administrative division. The anthropologist P. A. Talbot, who served as District Officer in charge of the Eket Division in 1910 and described the plays and masquerades of this area in some detail, makes no reference to Ugbom.

39. Mau masquerade, Nri-Awka Ibo. Helmet mask for fierce character called Mgbedike.

5
The Northern Ibo and their neighbours

The Northern Ibo

The main centre of Lower Niger sculpture and of many other crafts was located in the concentration of independent towns of migratory traders and craftsmen which, for lack of a common name, has been given that of its two most prominent towns, Nri and Awka. Men from this area, but particularly from these two places, travelled and traded among the people living on both sides of the Lower Niger. The chief speciality of the men of Nri derived from the mystical power of their ritual head, the Eze Nri, which they believed enabled them to remove and destroy other cults and medicines. The men of Awka were renowned as blacksmiths and woodcarvers and also as doctors and diviners.

Some Nigerian historians have associated the Igbo Uku burial and treasure with an early Eze Nri, but more definite evidence is needed to confirm this. Awka carvers were valued for their doors, stools, bowls and other utilitarian objects and for their style of decorative carving on panels and other smooth surfaces. Most of the masks and figures whose provenance is known, and particularly the helmet masks and Ikenga figures, were made by carvers in other neighbouring towns like Nimo, Nibo and Amobia, as well as from those further afield like Achalla. Besides woodcarving, the Nri-Awka area produced the finest of Ibo pots, the town of Inyi in particular specialising in the making of decorated pottery valued throughout the region for ceremonial purposes.

In their masquerades the beautiful female characters wore simple face masks with a headdress of coloured wools and ribbons wound around an openwork structure of cane or wire, or helmet masks in which the head portion represented a crested hair arrangement with bells, combs and other attachments (cover). These were attached to a tight-fitting costume embroidered with red, green and other bright-coloured threads made originally only in the Nri-Awka area for a masquerade called Ogbugulu Mau. Helmet masks were a Nri-Awka speciality found nowhere else except amongst the Northern Edo. Those representing fierce and dangerous spirits were a combination of tusks and horns and other animal features and were called Mgbedike (figure 39), Agunechenye and other impressive names. Other helmet masks combined the representation of a sun helmet with a masculine

40. Mau masquerade, Nri-Awka Ibo. Character called Oyibo (the white man).

face for a character called Ogaranya (big man) or, if given a cavalry moustache and costumed in a white drill suit, became Oyibo (figure 40), the white man. This was a new character, probably introduced soon after the 1914-18 war, which became immediately popular and spread very quickly to masquerades in other Ibo areas. Antelope, goats and similar animal spirits were given head masks and those with long muzzles were called Oji Onu (long mouth) or Ulaga (figure 25). Some animals (for example, Tortoise) were carved as a complete figure which was worn on the actor's head. There was a range of masks in various shapes, sizes, styles and materials representing comic, stupid and other human and animal types. There were also faceless characters where the actor's own face was concealed under a cloth or raffia hood. Some of these were said to be very old and senior, others were abstractions like the spirit called Government or three raffia-covered characters who sang together in thirds and were called Onukamma (the tongue is stronger than the sword). Some of the masks used in Nri-Awka masquerades were borrowed from elsewhere, mainly from the Ibibio.

Single figures, apart from a few animal ones, were absent from these Nri-Awka masquerades as were heads, whether human or animal. Combinations of figures arranged in a tableau and carried on the actor's head were occasionally used and among the Northern Ibo in the Nsukka division there was a masquerade they called Ekwe in which the actors bore on their heads a large pyramidal arrangement of human and animal figures piled one on top of the other. Achalla and a number of other Nri-Awka towns carried this idea a stage further by making very large 12-15 foot (3.7-4.6 metre) high structures decorated with cloth figures, coloured cloths, ribbons and streamers, which they called Ijele.

Most of the Northern Ibo towns called their masquerades and the characters that appeared in them Mau (ghost), though a few did not, notably the Ibo Odo and the Ibo Omabe. These were two groups of towns that had their own particular cult and masquerade, after which they were called: Odo and Omabe were said to be nature spirits of the surrounding waste land. In each town's ritual the spirit and a number of other masked or hooded characters were brought by the society to visit the town and, after being paraded round it, were returned to their home in the bush.

The Northern Ibo, but particularly the Nri-Awka, made the usual range of carved figures. There were tall, free-standing ones representing some of their tutelary deities; there were dolls and Agu Nsi, the familiars of diviners; and in the case of the Nri-Awka there were a very large number of Ikenga, which, as already mentioned, were made in all manner of styles and sizes.

Related areas: Western Ibo and Edo
Few masks and figures have been collected from the Western Ibo and the Ishan Edo. The Southern Edo and their Western Ibo neighbours were more prolific, as were the Northern or Kukuruku Edo, who seem to have drawn much of their inspiration from the Nri-Awka area. Both Edo and Western Ibo shared the Ikenga cult with the Northern and Southern Ibo. Western Ibo, bordering the Southern Edo, shared the Ivhri cult and its figures with their Edo and Ijo neighbours and carved other human figures for their household shrines, all of which carried the broad vertical gashes

on their foreheads which originally distinguished people of this area but are no longer found on the living. They had a masquerade called Ekeleke in which the characters performed on stilts and another called Ogonya in which the characters wore rattles on their ankles with which they stamped out a rhythm in time to the band. Their headpieces consisted of human or bird heads and of twin figures held together by an animal with its feet resting on the two heads (figure 27). They also had a trophy dance around a many-figured emblem called Nwamuo (figure 34). Very similar constructions were used by the Northern Edo, who carved helmet masks similar to those of the Nri-Awka. The Northern Edo also had a masquerade with multi-figured head-dresses similar to those of the Northern Ibo Ekwe. More recently (about 1920) they have copied the Ogbugulu Mau costumes, similar to those of the Nsukka area of the Northern Ibo, in which the mask is of cloth and part of the costume.

Idoma sculpture

Among the northern neighbours of the Ibo, the Idoma people carved white-faced masks very similar to those of the Nri-Awka, as well as figures seated on circular stools. Most of these Idoma masks can be distinguished from those of the Northern Ibo by their more rounded cheeks and by their possession of keloids arranged in vertical rows, one on each temple and one in the centre of the forehead. Nri-Awka masks prefer representations of 'Itchi marks' on the forehead of masks and figures representing male characters and many carry the distinguishing Nri-Awka curved triangles painted diagonally on the cheeks and sometimes repeated on the forehead (figure 10). One occasionally finds arrangements of keloids on Nri-Awka masks, while few Ohuhu-Ngwa Ibo and Ibibio masks are without them.

6
The Southern, Cross River and North-eastern Ibo

The Southern Ibo

The Southern Ibo were originally contained in the area between the Orashi and Sombreiro rivers in the west and the Imo River in the east, which consisted of a flat peneplain that sloped gradually southwards until it lost itself in the swamps of the Eastern Delta. Overseas access to this region was through the estuary that the Portuguese called the Rio Real and later traders the Bonny River, which formed the common embouchure of the New Calabar River and of other creeks that connected it with the Imo and the Sombreiro. It was these rivers, together with the Cross River further east, which in the nineteenth century evacuated the region's most valuable export, palm oil, and which, when it came under British control, gave it its first colonial name of the Oil Rivers Protectorate.

In the north bordering the Nri-Awka Ibo were the Western Isuama Ibo, very similar in their culture and economic organisation. In the south along the Delta margin were two non-Ibo groups speaking Cross River languages, the Abua and the Ogoni, each with their own masquerades and art styles. Between them were the Oratta, Etche and Ikwerre Ibo and along the Orashi and Sombreiro rivers were the riverain Ibo tribes of Oba and Ekpeya. Ikwerre expansion southward had carried them to the Delta margin, forcing the Abua across the Sombreiro River and establishing contact on the New Calabar with the Ijo group which, when it moved down to the Rio Real, became the trading state of Kalabari. Other Ibo groups had settled on the eastern side of the Lower Imo as the Asa and, in combination with Ijo migrants, the Ndokki tribes. Some of these Ndokki Ijo later moved down to the Rio Real and settled below the Kalabari as the state of Ubani or Bonny.

Ibo expansion, however, was mainly on the part of the Isuama, who spread westwards to the Imo and then across it to the Umuahia area of the Bende administrative division. This became a major diffusion centre with Ibo spreading southwards to become the Ngwa, eastward to the Middle Cross River and north-eastwards into the plains beyond, absorbing any Ibibio and Middle Cross River elements already there and developing into

the Cross River and North-eastern Ibo. The high ground between
the Cross River and its tributary the Enyong seems to have been
an expansion area from which people dispersed: first Ibibio
expanding westwards towards the Imo and later the Ada group of
Cross River Ibo who moved northwards out of the forest country.
Amongst those that remained behind or who moved to the area
later were the group of villages that became the Arochuku tribe.
With the development of their trading organisation, Bende in the
Ohuhu area became their principal market for receiving slaves
that came from further north and distributing them between the
slave markets of the three trading states on the Delta margin and
the Lower Cross River.

Slaves had to walk overland by the most direct routes, but palm
oil had to travel in bulk and therefore by water, so when it
became Nigeria's principal export the Oil Rivers and those Ibo
who were able to use them came into their own. The Aro lost
their monopoly of the inland trade to other Ibo groups, notably
the Western Isuama, and to Cross River Ibo groups like the Item
and the Abiriba. The Kalabari extended their oil markets up the
Orashi and Sombreiro rivers, while the Bonny traders carried
theirs up the Imo and its tributaries. By the end of the century
they had, together with the overseas firms with which they
traded, removed themselves from the Rio Real to establish the
new ports of Abonnema and Opobo where these rivers entered
the Delta. This development and realignment of trade was
reflected in the recreational activities of the people and as in the
days of the overseas slave trade there seems to have been
considerable correlation between the distribution of trade and of
masquerades and of the societies that organised them. These
were not the only factors affecting them. Different communities
had very different attitudes towards innovation or conservation
and this was affected again by their remoteness from or proximity
to the rapid social changes that accompanied the end of the
nineteenth century.

Ibo masks and figures show none of the uniformity of form and
style that characterise the Yoruba sculpture of Western Nigeria.
This diversity becomes apparent as soon as we study their
distribution. A survey made in the 1930s showed that, while the
Northern Ibo masquerades used face and helmet masks and
rarely employed heads, the Southern Ibo shared with Ijo and
Cross River masquerades a preference for heads and head masks
and an avoidance of face masks. The Western Isuama Ibo, who
are in many respects the southern half of the Nri-Awka, used

41. (Left) Ajonku masquerade, Abiriba town, Cross River Ibo. Skin-covered head called Ajonku. Note the ancient Indian cotton print displayed with it.

42. (Right) Ekpe (Ibo) head, Ngwa Ibo, from extinct Ekpe (Ibo) masquerade. Now in Nigerian National Museum, Lagos.

heads and face masks, often in combination. Although this preference for heads extended over the whole of the Southern Ibo area, it is in most other respects divided by the Imo River into two distinct cultural areas or sectors, a Western or Owerri sector and an Eastern or Umuahia.

   Once they had crossed the Imo the Ibo left behind them their Ofo, Ikenga and other personal cults, changed the names of some of their deities and incorporated Cross River ones into their pantheon. Those that became the Cross River Ibo looked to the Middle Cross River and the trading state at its mouth for many of their social and cultural institutions. So, though to a lesser extent, did the Ohuhu-Ngwa Ibo. The Ohuhu were in the centre of the Arochuku trading organisation. Slaves from Bende market were routed through the Ngwa country to the Bonny markets in Ndokki on the Lower Imo and in the nineteenth century Ohuhu-Ngwa oil went down the same river to its Delta port of

43. Okorosie masquerade, Eziama town, Western Isuama Ibo. Onyejuwe (Spellbound) and another 'beautiful' female character.

Opobo. The Arochuku had adopted the Ekpe (Egbo) secret society of Old Calabar with all its grades. Most of the Ohuhu villages also had this society but with subordinate grades of Akang and Okonko. These grades had a masquerade, also called Okonko, with characters that rushed about in tight-fitting net costumes called, in Old Calabar, 'Egbo runners' (figure 29). They also had other masquerades with skin-covered heads, the older ones depicting a character, said to be male, called Ajonku (figure 41), the more recent depicting a female character with a long neck and exaggerated 'horns' called Ikem (figure 5) and a fierce male one with a Janus shoulder mask (figure 28). The Ohuhu, the Ngwa and the Ndokki also carved plain wooden heads in a number of different styles for an ancient masquerade (figure 42), now defunct in Ohuhu, that they called Ekpe — distinguished elsewhere in this volume as Ekpe (Ibo) — and later they borrowed from further west the Ekeleke masquerade in which the characters danced on stilts and wore heads carved and painted in a very modern style. They also had masks, many of them bought or copied from the Ibibio. They called them Isi Ekpo (Ekpo Face) and used them in masquerades which they either called Ekpe, and which were probably a variation of the original Ekpe (Ibo), or they kept the original Ibibio name of Ekpo.

Apart from occasional Agu Nsi figures used by diviners, the carving of figures in the Ohuhu-Ngwa sector was confined to the Ugbom used in the trophy dance of the same name, which they had originally borrowed from the Ibibio but now carved in a number of local styles. The dance is no longer performed but a number of the figures have survived, most of which are now in the Nigerian National Museum.

In the Owerri sector interest in masquerades was concentrated in the Western Isuama towns and in the communities bordering the Orashi and Sombreiro rivers that sold their oil to the Kalabari traders at Abonnema. The Eastern Isuama, at least in the 1930s, were not interested in masquerades and their sculpture was

44. Okorosie masquerade, Eziama town, Western Isuama Ibo. 'Beautiful' mask called Nwanyure (Proud Woman) and 'fierce' mask called Akatakpuru. He carries a gong; the light-coloured palm fronds around his waist warn of his dangerous supernatural power.

45. Ekeleke masquerade, Orsu tribe, Western Isuama Ibo. The characters are dancing on stilts.

mainly confined to family groups of figures for the shrines of their local deities, while most of the Oratta and Etche Ibo concentrated their creative energies on mud sculpture for bigger and better Mbari houses.

The Western Isuama had developed a local style of face masks and heads representing a range of characters very similar to those of the Nri-Awka masquerades. There was a greater variation and elaboration of the 'beautiful' white-faced masks, many being combined with one or more heads and sometimes carved as a single piece (figures 43 and 44). The usual name for the masquerade was Okorosie but it was also called Owu and, more rarely, Okonko. Owu is the Ijo name for a water spirit and the characters in these masquerades were said to be spirits of this sort. Okonko, as mentioned previously, was a Cross River type of masquerade and in the Ohuhu area from where this name was derived its characters were said to be the servants of Ekpe, a forest demon. However, the characters and supporting masks in these Isuama masquerades, whether they were called Okorosie, Owu or Okonko, remained the same and were drawn from local mythology and from contemporary life. None of them, except possibly a white-faced, 'beautiful' mask called DC (District Commissioner) and another called Miri Osimiri (Sea Bird), who was his wife, could be said to have any connection with water. (In Ibo mythology Europeans are said to come from the sea.)

Although the Owu/Okorosie/Okonko type of masquerade was the principal Western Isuama masquerade they also had another, said to have been introduced more recently from further west (figure 45). This was called Ekeleke and the characters, who all wore white-faced female heads or in some cases heads and torsos, danced on stilts and would appear to have been the same as the

46. Owu masquerade, Ekpeya tribe, Riverain Ibo. Mask called Ohwa with a hinged lower jaw.

47. Ogbukele masquerade, Ekpeya tribe, Riverain Ibo. Head mask for character representing a 'were' hippopotamus. Now in the Liverpool Museum.

Ekeleke masquerade of the Isoko Edo, the neighbouring Western Ibo and the Ohuhu masquerade of this name.

Further south among the Egbema and Oba villages the masquerade was called Owu. It had much the same characters but a greater range of face masks and heads, some carved in the Isu Ama style, some their own invention, and some with hinged lower jaws (figure 46), twisted mouths and noses and other features borrowed from Ibibio and Ogoni masks. They had also borrowed from the Central Ijo masquerades the use of figures as masks.

Their southern neighbours, the Ekpeya (sometimes called the Ekpaffia), also had this Owu masquerade with the same range of characters, face masks and figures carved in the same style, but they had in addition adopted the Ogbukele secret society of the Abua people (who lay between them and the Kalabari). With it had come the society meeting house, drum, Ogbukele masquerade and very different characters and masks representing water animal and predatory fish spirits with highly conventionalised head masks and figures (figures 47, 48 and 49). These were the first and only true Owu spirits produced by these masquerades, but they had to share the Ekpeya masquerade with

48. Owu masquerade, Rumuji town, Southern Ikwerre Ibo. Figure of a fierce fish spirit called Abbam.

49. Owu masquerade, Rumuji town, Southern Ikwerre Ibo. Heads of four beautiful female characters called (above left) Oyi Aro (Aro Face); (above right) Mammywata (Mermaid); (below left) Nwere Utobo (wife of Utobo); (below right), Ogalanya (Bright and Shining).

50. Okwanku masquerade, Akanu town, Ohaffia tribe, Cross River Ibo. Dibia (Doctor) with his bag of medicines, Onyechumiri (Rain Driver) with gum boots and broom to drive the rain away and, in begrimed straw hat, Obaji (Chin Beard). Dibia, having poisoned Onyechumiri, is now trying to revive him.

birds and land animals (dogs, pangolins, tortoises and so on, represented by figures in a naturalistic style) and with two characters wearing conventionalised male heads who were said to be the first and second Heads of Ogbukele. The Ikwerre on the New Calabar River had the same type of masquerade with the same range of characters but called Owu. In this case the Head of Owu was a character wearing a face mask and draped in a costume of raffia fringes, probably to indicate antiquity. The other characters in this, as in the other Ogbukele, Owu and Okorosie masquerades, wore drapes of imported cotton cloths.

While the Northern Ibo shared with the Yoruba, Edo and Igala the general name of 'ghost' (Egwu, Egungu, Mau) for their masquerades and had what amounted to a single cultural centre in the Nri-Awka towns from which to derive their titles, societies, masquerades, cult figures and other sculpture, there was no such uniformity amongst the Southern Ibo. In the case of their masquerades and other sculpture there are some that would seem to be a local invention ancient enough to be supported by a traditional style of sculpture, like the Western Isuama and Oba masquerades now called Okorosie and Owu, the Ekpe (Ibo) of the Ohuhu-Ngwa Ibo or, if we include non-Ibo groups, the Ogubukele society and masquerade of the Abua. However, there were others that were brought in from outside, from the Cross River in the case of Ekpe (Egbo) and Ikem, from the Delta in the case of the Owu/Okorosie group, from the Southern Edo and Western Ibo in the case of Ekeleke and from the Ibibio in the case of the Isi Ekpo masks and the Ugbom trophy dance. Some of these intrusions came without any change, like Ekeleke and Ikem, but most changed gradually as they moved. The Old Calabar Ekpe (Egbo) was taken over with all its grades by the Arochuku villages. In the Ohuhu Ekpe (Egbo) there were only two grades, Akang and Okonko, and occasionally a third called Obon. Beyond the Imo on the western side all that was left was the name of one of these grades, Okonko. Similarly the Abuan Ogbukele type of Owu masquerade was taken over in its entirety by the Ekpeya but only the names Owu and Okorosie penetrated further inland, where they replaced the original names of the traditional masquerades.

Individual masks and characters travelled further and more erratically, being brought back by travellers and traders and introduced as new characters into their home masquerades. The 'Egbo runner' costume found its way northward into a northern Ibo Mau masquerade as Traveller (figure 29). An Ibibio pathological mask appeared in the Eziama (Western Isuama) Okorosie as the character called Lawyer, its twisted mouth indicating the true function of a lawyer, which according to Ibo mythology was to 'twist the truth'.

The Cross River Ibo

This group of Ibo divides into two culturally distinct groups. Those in the south were more involved in trade and travelling, particularly the Arochuku and the Abiriba. The Arochuku were too widely scattered and absent from their home villages to have much time for sculpture and dramatic entertainment. This was left to the Abiriba and the Ohaffia. Both had Ekpe (Egbo) and its masquerades but, unlike the Arochuku and like the northern group, they had retained their original system of village government, which was based on their age organisation. Their meeting houses, which in other parts of the Cross River belonged exclusively to the men of the village and to their Ekpe (Egbo) society, became among the Abiriba and Ohaffia villages the village or ward meeting house dedicated to its tutelary spirit and

51. Ceremonial drum, Abiriba town, Cross River Ibo, said to have been carved by Ibibio, but obviously carved locally.

52. Ngbangba Ikoro masquerade, Abiriba town, Cross River Ibo. Masked band.

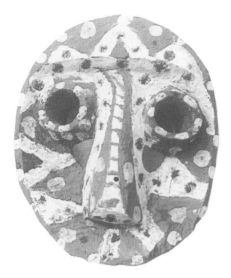

53. Lughulu masquerade. Item tribe, Isu-Item Ibo. Comic face mask.

open to its women as well as its men, with the secret paraphernalia of the society stored in two rooms at the back. The pillars of
these houses were finely carved and in Abiriba and in Asaga
Ohaffia town carved figures were attached to them and to the side
walls. These were said to represent the spirit servants of the deity
(figure 11). Their carvers made both skin-covered and plain
wooden heads and masks and looked particularly to the Ibibio for
their ideas. Some of the Ohaffia towns had masquerades and
masks peculiar to them. In the Akanu town Okwanku masquerade the characters acted together in a comic drama in which
the character called Dibia (Doctor) poisoned the one called Rain
Driver and then brought him back to life again (figure 50).

Abiriba was, like Awka, a town of traders and craftsmen, with
travelling doctors, diviners, blacksmiths and carvers of masks and
figures in either a local Abiriba style or in what they insisted was
Ibibio. Others made ornamental bowls and dishes, drums (figure
51) and other objects. More recently they have introduced a
system of resist-dyeing of imported baft cloth (called Ukara). In
the 1930s their principal masquerade, called Ngbangba Ikoro,
had a band of twenty or more small boys and young men wearing
masks that looked like face masks but were worn on top of their
heads and playing on clappers and metal gongs of various sizes
(figure 52). The characters in this masquerade consisted of two
clowns with masks worn over their faces and a principal dancer
called Otiri with a mask worn on top of his head and stuck full of

54. Ifogu masquerade, Nkporo tribe, Cross River Ibo. Hooded character with headdress of birds' feathers and a rosette of cowrie shells, attached to a netted bag with streamer ends that can be pulled out in front in order to see the way. He has to be sewn into his costume of raffia sacking for each performance.

55. Ifogu masquerade, Nkporo tribe, Cross River Ibo. The actor is impersonating a fashion-conscious young woman and wears a tight-fitting cotton blouse and bead necklace.

long feathers, his face shrouded in a raffia bag, and wearing a shirt of raffia sacking and a grass skirt. His right arm and left leg were painted in white chalk (Nzu) and the other arm and leg in yellow (Odo). The 'copyright' in this play and its masks was vested in a family of carvers. If one of them carved a mask for sale he had to share the proceeds with his brother carvers. There were a number of other masquerades, each belonging to a particular section of the community. One was called Okwanku and was said to be similar to the Ohaffia one. Abiriba men who traded in the Ibibio country had their own society and masquerade called Ekpo Ibibio with elaborate masks said to have been obtained from the Ibibio, which appeared and danced at a member's funeral. There were also Cross River types of masquerade with characters wearing skin-covered heads, a fierce one called Ajonku (figure 41) and a 'beautiful' long-necked female one called Ikarum that danced at weddings.

Neighbouring villages like those of the Item and Alayi had their own selection of masquerades and trophy dances, some with skin-covered heads, some with face masks. Some of these conformed to a generalised Cross River or Ibo style, others had their own local variations. Thus, in the Item Lughulu masquerade there were two characters with face masks reduced in size (like those of the Ada group of Cross River Ibo) which left the lower jaw and neck of the actor exposed. One was male and comic

56. Isiji masquerade, Nkporo tribe, Cross River Ibo. Initiates all have similar masks of coloured strips of raffia stretched over a cane frame and attached to a calabash face mask. They are draped in young palm fronds which are thought to carry magical powers.

57. Ifogu masquerade, Nkporo tribe, Cross River Ibo. Mask called Mba. The character is distinguished by his eagle feather.

(figure 53), the other 'beautiful' and female. In the Lughulu masquerade of Ugwueke Alayi town there were a number of characters all wearing masks of the same style and of full size (figure 8).

The Ada group

The northern tribes of Cross River Ibo, usually distinguished as the Ada group after the name of their principal tribe, had their own very distinctive styles of mask, some of them similar to other Ibo masks but most of them unique (figures 4, 54 and 57). Almost all of them were reduced in size and covered only the upper part of the wearer's face. Like the southern group these tribes were organised on an age-grade basis but in their case with a very elaborate system of initiation for the subgrades in the junior grade. Associated with these rituals were a series of masquerades which varied slightly between each tribe. Those of the Afikpo tribes have been described in detail by S. Ottenberg in *Masked Rituals of Afikpo* (1975). In Ngusu, the senior Ada town, the junior grade was divided into the subgrades of small boys

(Umuerima), Isiji and Isiugo. The first two had their Egede and Isiji masquerades, which they were entitled to perform after they had passed their initiation. In these they all wore the same type of mask made out of a calabash, which in Isiji was given a tall superstructure of leaves and raffia (figure 56). The most rigorous initiation took place in Isiugu, after which the initiates passed into the middle grade and were entitled to perform the Item Mbe masquerade wearing masks called Mba or Opa Ada (figure 57) and to participate in all the other Ngusu masquerades. These were numerous, some with face masks in the local style, like Ikwumocha (figure 58), others, like Asi Uku, with skin-covered heads. In the Nkporo tribe the masquerade was called Ifogu. The Mba masks were the same but the costumes differed.

The Ada group carved few figures apart from those used by diviners as their Agu Nsi. Their meeting houses were relatively crude in construction and had no rooms. The Item Mbe and other masks were kept under the roof, stuck into the thatch, and the houses were therefore barred to women.

58. Ifogu masquerade, Nkporo tribe, Cross River Ibo. Face mask in the form of a parrot's beak for character called Ikwumocha.

The North-eastern Ibo

In contrast to the Cross River Ibo, the North-eastern Ibo were in general much less involved in masquerading and sculpture. Most of their craftsmen came from the Ezza tribe, who were the local blacksmiths and had carvers who made bowls, platters, dishes and slit drums (gongs), some of them of considerable refinement. The Ezza and the Izi also carved dolls and other figures (figure 59). Few masquerades were being performed in this region in the 1930s and the North-eastern Ibo seem to have developed no recognisable style of their own, apart from a highly conventionalised Elephant head mask called Obodo Enyi (figure 60); the masquerade in which it performed has been described for the Yako and other Middle Cross River peoples.

The Ngbo and Ezengbo tribes in the north of the area borrowed the Egwu (Mau) masquerade of their Agala (Idoma) neighbours and the Izi tribe had a masquerade, Okperegede, that

59. Figure of mother and child, Ezza tribe, North-eastern Ibo.

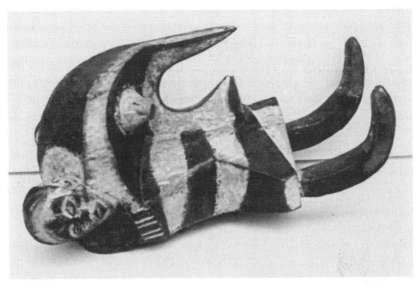

60. Obodo Enyi age set masquerade, Izi tribe, North-eastern Ibo. Obodo Enyi mask represents a 'were' elephant.

was found in most Izi and Ikwo villages. Today there has been a resurgence of interest in masquerading, though the masks and heads used in these revived masquerades seem to be borrowed or copied from elsewhere. In one Okperegede, for example, the principal character, Asufu, wore a modern Cross River type of Janus shoulder mask (no longer covered with skin but painted in oils), the white-faced female and clown masks were borrowed from other Ibo areas, the head worn by Onyeocha (White Man) was carved in a naturalistic Ibibio style and the horned white-faced head for Orumpi could have come from an Ohuhu masquerade.

7
Museums

The following are some of the museums that have collections of Ibo art. Not all of it will be on display and anyone wishing to study the whole collection is advised to write to the curator in advance to find out if it can be made available at short notice.

Great Britain
Cambridge University Museum of Archaeology and Anthropology, Downing Street, Cambridge CB2 3DZ. Telephone: 0233 337733 or 33516.
Liverpool Museum, William Brown Street, Liverpool, Merseyside L3 8EN. Telephone: 051-207 0001 or 5451.
Museum of Mankind (The Ethnography Department of the British Museum), 6 Burlington Gardens, London WIX 2EX. Telephone: 01-323 8043.
Pitt Rivers Museum, South Parks Road, Oxford OX1 3PP. Telephone: 0865 270927.
Royal Museum of Scotland, Chambers Street, Edinburgh EH1 1JF. Telephone: 031-225 7534.

Europe
Musée d'Ethnographie, Boulevard Carl Vogt 65 - 7, 1205 Geneva, Switzerland.
Musée de l'Homme, Palais de Chaillot, Place du Trocadéro, 75016 Paris, France.
Musée Royal de l'Afrique Centrale, Leuvensesteenweg 13, 1980 Tervuren, Belgium.
Museum für Völkerkunde, Arnimallee 23-27, 1000 Berlin 33, West Germany.
Museum für Völkerkunde, Heldenplatz 3, Neue Hofburg, 1010 Vienna 1, Austria.
Museum für Völkerkunde, Schaumainkai 29, 6000 Frankfurt am Main, West Germany.
Museum für Völkerkunde, Taubchenweg 2, 7010 Leipzig, East Germany.
Museum Rietberg, Gablerstrasse 15, 8002 Zürich, Switzerland.

Nigeria
National Museum of Nigeria, Department of Antiquities, Onikan, Lagos.

North America

American Museum of Natural History, 79th Street and Central Park West, New York, NY 10024, USA.

Brooklyn Museum, 188 Eastern Parkway, New York, NY 11238, USA.

Buffalo Museum of Science, Humboldt Parkway, Buffalo, New York 14211, USA.

Cleveland Museum of Art, 11150 East Boulevard, Cleveland, Ohio 44106, USA.

Dallas Museum of Fine Arts, Fair Park, Dallas, Texas 75226, USA.

The Denver Art Museum, 100 West 14th Avenue Parkway, Denver, Colorado 80204, USA.

Field Museum of Natural History, Roosevelt Road and Lake Shore Drive, Chicago, Illinois 60605, USA.

The High Museum of Art, 1280 Peachtree Street NE, Atlanta, Georgia 30309, USA.

Indiana University Art Museum, Fine Arts Building, Bloomington, Indiana 47405, USA.

Metropolitan Museum of Art, 5th Avenue at 82nd Street, New York, NY 10028, USA.

Museum of Cultural History, Haines Hall, University of California, Los Angeles, California 90024, USA.

National Museum of African Art, 950 Independence Avenue SW, Washington DC 20560, USA.

Robert H. Lowie Museum of Anthropology, 103 Kroeber Hall, University of California, Berkeley, California 94720, USA.

Royal Ontario Museum, 100 Queen's Park, Toronto, Ontario M5C 2C6, Canada.

Seattle Art Museum, Volunteer Park, Seattle Center, Seattle, Washington 98112, USA.

Stanford University Museum and Art Gallery, Museum Way, Stanford, California 94305, USA.

University Museum, University of Pennsylvania, 33rd and Spruce Streets, Philadelphia, Pennsylvania 19104, USA.

University of Michigan Museum of Art, 525 South State Street, Ann Arbor, Michigan 48109, USA.

Vancouver Museum, 1100 Chestnut Street, Vancouver, British Columbia, Canada.

8
Further reading

Ibo art
Cole, H. M., and Aniakor, C. G. *Igbo Arts: Community and Cosmos.* Museum of Cultural History, University of California, Los Angeles, 1984.
Jones, G. I. *The Art of Eastern Nigeria.* Cambridge University Press, 1984.

Antique Ibo bronzes
Shaw, Thurstan. *Unearthing Ibo Uku.* Oxford University Press, Ibadan, 1977.

Ibo mud sculpture
Cole, H. M. *Mbari.* Indiana University Press, Bloomington, Indiana, 1982.

Ikenga cult figures
Boston, J. S. *Ikenga Figures.* Federal Department of Antiquities, Nigeria, in association with Ethnographica, London, 1977.

Afikpo Ibo masks
Ottenberg, S. *Masked Rituals of Afikpo.* University of Washington Press, Seattle and London, 1975.

Nigerian art
Ekpo, Eyo. *2000 Years of Nigerian Art.* Federal Department of Antiquities, Nigeria, 1974.
Elisophon, Eliot. *The Sculpture of Africa.* Thames and Hudson, 1958.
Fagg, W. *Nigerian Images.* Lund Humphries, 1963.

Index

Page numbers in italic refer to illustrations.

Abaja tribe 26
Abam tribe 38
Abbam 56
Abiriba tribe 6, 12, 26, 38, 50, 59, 61, 62
Aboh town 43
Abonnema port 8, 50, 53
Abua tribe 49, 56, 59
Achalla town 45, 47
Ada group 36, 50, 64, 65
Adze 11
Afikpo tribe 64
Agala tribe 66
Agar Collection 44
Age grades 64
Agunechenyi 45
Agu Nsi 38, 39, 47, 53, 65
Ahoada Division 5
Ajonku 51, 52
Akang 52
Akatakpuru 53
Akwete town 12
Alayi tribe 63
Ale 23, 24, 37
Amobia town 45
Anambara: river 5
  state 5
Ancestor cults 34, 37
Ancestors 34
Ane 37
Armlets and anklets, ivory 19
Aro 6, 50
Arochuku 6, 50, 51, 59
Arrowheads 26
Asaga town 61
Asa tribe 49
Ashanti stool 30
Asi Uku 65
Asufu 67
Awka: carvers 45
  stool 30
  town 26, 45, 61
Awo Olia 35
Axes 11
Ayaka 34
Bags 12
Barbers 14
Basins 12
Baskets 12
  market 12, 13, 28
Beads 18
  Cambay 19
  Igbo Uku 18
Bells 14
  brass 26
Benches 27
Bende: division 49
  tribe 50, 51
Bendel state 5
Benin 26
  kingdom 26
Benue river 6
Biafran War 5
Bird: figures 39, 42, 58
  heads 48
Blacksmiths 5, 11, 45, 61, 66
Body: painting 15, 18, 22, 23, 27
  scarring 14
Bonny: river 6, 49
  state 6, 49, 50, 51
Bottles, wooden 28, 28

Bowls 45, 61, 66
  Okwa Nzu (chalk) 27, 28
  pottery 20
  wooden 26
Boxes 27
Brasswork 26
'Brer Rabbit' 34
Calabar 6
  New 6
  Old 6, 8, 36, 52, 59
  river 49, 58
Calabash 23
  mask 63, 64
Cameroons 12
Camwood 12
Cap guns 26
Carvers 5, 61, 66
  Awka 45
  wood 45
Carving: bottles 28
  chalk bowl 27
  doors 25
  figure 10
  hand mirror 27
  ivory 19
  Nri-Awka 13
  panel 45
  stools 29
Cement figures 21, 21
Chair 27
Chalk 15
Chisel 11
Christian evangelism 8
Chuku 37
Clappers 61
Cloth, cotton 12, 58
Clothing 13
  second-hand 12
Clover, four-leaf 28
Clubs 26
Combs 14, 26
Compounds 24
Congo 12
Cotton, weaving 12
Cross River 5, 18, 20, 26, 34, 39, 49, 50, 59, 63
  languages 49
  Lower 50
  Middle 49, 51
Currency 26
Cutlass 11
Dagger 11
Dance: emblem 51
  fertility 39
  trophy 41
  Ugbom 39
  war 39
Decking 27
Deity: personal 38
  tutelary 38, 39
Delta 34, 49, 50, 59
  Eastern 5, 49
Demon, forest 54
Dibia 58, 61
Dish 61, 66
  ceremonial 28
  wooden 26
District Commissioner (DC) 55
Diviner 37, 38, 45, 47, 61
Doctor 45, 61
Dogs 58
Doll 47, 66

Door 26
  carved 25, 26, 45
Dress 12
Drum 40, 61
  Abiriba 60
  Ikoro 26, 40
  Ogbukele 22, 56
  slit (gong) 23, 26, 66
Eastern Delta 5
Eastern Railway 20
Eastern Region 26
Economy, domestic 11
Edo 5, 12, 30, 40, 47, 55, 58
  Northern 9, 36, 45, 47, 48
  Southern 9, 17, 24, 41, 47, 59
Efik tribe 6, 35
Egbema tribe 56
Egbo Brass 36
  runner 35, 36, 38, 52, 59
Egede 65
Egungu 58
Egwu 58, 66
Ekeleke 48, 52, 54, 55, 59
Eket 8, 44
  tribe 44
Ekoi tribe 35
Ekpaffia tribe 56
Ekpe 35, 52, 53, 54
  Egbo 35, 36, 52, 59
  Ibo 51, 52, 53, 59
  secret society 36
Ekpeya: stool 38
  tribe 24, 49, 56, 59
Ekpo 34, 53, 59
  Ibibio 62
Ekwe: headdress 32
  masquerade 47, 48
Elephant 66
Emblems 39
Enyong river 50
Etche tribe 25, 54
Europeans 55
Eze Nri 45
Eziama town 59
Ezza tribe 26, 66, 66
Facial marks 16, 48
  scarring 16
Ghost 34
Goat 46
God, High 37
Gong 23, 26, 61
'Government' 47
Guns: cap 26
  Dane 11
Hairdressing: horned 14
  moulded 14
Handles, wooden 26
Hat, top 12
Hausa 5
Head 31
  Ekpe (Ibo) 51
  Owu 55, 57
  rests 26
  skin-covered 51, 52, 59, 63, 65
Headdress 31
  twin-figured 34
Helmet: mask 31, 44, 45, cover
Hippopotamus 41
Historians, Nigerian 45

Hoods, raffia 47
Horn, ivory tusk 19, 40
Houses 21, 23, 24
  Mbari 23, 24, 25
  meeting 56, 59, 65
Ibibio 6, 8, 18, 23, 26, 33, 43, 47, 48, 49, 50, 53, 56, 59, 61, 62
  stool 30
  style 8, 42
Ibo 18, 36, 49
  Cross River or Eastern 5, 6, 12, 14, 18, 23, 24, 26, 36, 38, 40, 41, 49, 50, 51, 59, 63, 64, 65
  Isuama 17, 37
  Isu-Item 17
  North-eastern 5, 6, 20, 26, 28, 40, 50, 66
  Northern 5, 6, 12, 17, 24, 26, 28, 34, 36, 37, 39, 40, 45, 47, 48, 50, 58
  Nri-Awka 15, 18, 19, 37, 40, 45, 48, 49, 50
  Odo 47
  Ohuhu-Ngwa 18, 39, 40, 41, 48, 50, 51, 53, 59
  Omabe 47
  Riverain 47
  Southern 5, 6, 12, 17, 24, 30, 37, 39, 40, 47, 55, 59
  Western (Ika) 40, 41
  Western Isuama 49, 50
Ibudu 22
Idoma tribe 9, 18, 48
Ifogu 9, 12, 62, 62 64, 65
Igala tribe 9, 12, 40, 58
Igbo Uku 6, 17, 18, 26, 45
Ijebu Ode town 12
Ijele 47
Ijo 8, 47, 49, 50, 54
  Central 17, 56
Ika Ibo, Northern and Southern 34, 38, 41
Ikarum 62
Ikem 14, 52, 59
Ikenga 28, 38, 39, 40, 42, 45, 47, 50
Ikoro drum 26, 40
Ikwerre tribe 49, 56, 58
Ikwo tribe 66
Imo: river 49, 50, 51, 59
  river, Lower 13, 49, 51
  state 5
Indigo 12
Initiation 65
Inyi pottery 20, 45
Iron 25
  belled staff 26
  spears 26
Ishan (Edo) 15, 47
Ishiago pottery 20
Isi Ekpo 53, 59
Isiji and Isiugo 65
Isoko (Edo) 5, 59
Isuama Ibo 17, 27, 37, 49
  Eastern 37, 53
  Western 49, 50, 53, 54, 55, 58, 59
Isu-Item Ibo 16, 17, 42

Ibo Art

Isu tribe 36
Itchi marks *16*, 17, 48
Item Mbe 65
Item tribe 26, 50, 63
Ivhri 40, *43, 47*
Ivory: anklets, armlets, horns 19, *23*
Izi tribe 66
Jewellery 18
Jugs, European 21
Kalabari state and tribe 6, 49, 50, 53, 56
Keloids 18, *17, 41*, 48, *51*
Knives: hunting 11
  yam *42*
Knots, interlaced and endless 28
Kukuruku (Edo) 5, 47
Kwa Ibo river 44
Lagos 12
Lawyer 59
Leopard 35
  skin 39
Society, Human 35
Lughulu *16, 61*, 63
Map 7
Marks, facial, tribal 16, 18
Mask 27, 31, 45, 61
  animal 31
  beautiful 45, 54, 63
  bird 48, 56
  calabash 64
  cloth 48
  comic *61*
  dog 56
  elephant 66
  face *16, 18*, 50, 56, 58, 63
  female 45
  fierce 33
  figure *33, 55*
  goat 46
  head *33*, 50, 51, *55*, 56, 67
  helmet 31, *44*, 45, 48, 50, *cover*
  Isi Ekpo 52
  Isiji and Isiugo 64
  Janus 31, *35*, 67
  Mba *13, 64*, 64
  pangolin 56
  pathological 59
  shoulder 32, *35*, 67
  tortoise 33, *34*, 46, 56
Masquerades 31, 33
  age grade 64
  Cross River 62
  Ekeleke 48, 52, *54*, 56
  Ekpe (Egbo) 25, 35
  Ekpe (Ibo) 53, 58
  Ekpeya tribe 56
  Ekpo 53
  Ekpo Isi 53
  Ifogu *9, 12, 62, 64*, 65
  Ikem *14*, 59
  Isiji and Isiugo *63*, 65
  Isuama 54
  Item Mbe 65
  Lughulu *16, 61*, 63
  Mau *33, 35, 44, 46*, 47, 59
  Ngbangba Ikoro *60*, 61
  Nri-Awka 47
  Ogbugulu Mau 45, 48
  Ogbukele *55*, 56, 59
  Ogonya *34*, 48
  Okorosie *52, 53*, 54,

55, 56, 59
Okperegede 67
Okwanku *58*, 61, 62
Owu *10*, *33*, *55*, *56*, *57*, 58
  small boys 31, *32*
Matchet, farming and fighting 11
Mats, sleeping 12
Mau 34, 47, 58, 59
Mba *13, 64*, 65
Mbari 25, 54
  Southern Oratta *23*, *24*, 25, 37
  Ulakwo and Umuowa *23*
Meeting house *19*, 27
Metalwork 25, 26
Mgbedike *44*, 45
Miri Osimiri 55
Mirror, hand *27*, 28
Mo 34
Mortar 26
Murray, K. C. 43
Museum: Liverpool *55*
  of Mankind 21
  Nigerian National *51*, 53
  Wellcome *43*
Music, Ibo 22
Musical instruments 22, 23
Musical pots 21
Musket, flintlock 26
Mythology, Ibo 55, 59
Ndokki tribe 12, 49, 52
Ngbangba Ikoro *60*, 61
Ngbo tribe 12, 66
Ngusu town 64, 65
Ngwa tribe 51, 52
Nibo town 45
Niger: Cross River hinterland 5
  Lower 5, 8, 9, 18, 26, 38, 40
  Lower, style 9
  river 5, 28, 30
  sculpture 45
Nigeria: Eastern 36
  Western 50
Nimo town 45
Nkwerri town 26
Nri-Awka Ibo 15, 20, 26
  masquerades 47, 48
Nri town 45
Nsukka: area 48
  division 47
Nupe: designs 28
  stools 56
Nwamuo dance 32, 39, *41*, 48
Nwanyure *53*
Nze *16*
Obaji *58*
Oba tribe 49, 56, 58
Obodo Enyi 66, *67*
Obon 59
Obu house *19*
Odo 47
Ofo 51
  anthropomorphic 37
Ogaranya 46
Ogbugulu Mau 45, 48, 56, 58, 59
Ogbukele drum *22*
Ogoni tribe 33, 49, 56
Ogonya *34*, 48
Ogume town *41*

Ohaffia tribe 26, 38, 59, 61, 62
Ohuhu-Ngwa Ibo 39, 41, 48, 51, 53, 59
Ohuhu tribe 51, 52, 56, 59, 67
Ohwa *55*
Oil palm 49
Oil Rivers 50
  Protectorate 8, 49
Oji Onu 46
Okigwi 26
Okonko 52, 54, 55, 59
Okorosie *52, 53*, 54, 55, 56, 59
Okperegede 67
Okwanku 25, *58*
Omabe 47
Onitsha province 5
Onukamma 47
Onyechumiri *58*
Onyejuwe *52*
Onyeocha 67
Opa Ada 64
Opobo: gown 12, *21*
  town 8, 50, 52
Orashi river 49, 50, 54
Oratta tribe 25, 37, 49, 54
Ornaments 40
Orsu tribe 39, *54*
Orumpi 67
Osissa town 20
Ottenberg, S. 64
Owerri: province 5
  town 51, 53
Owu 34, 54, 55, 56, 58, 59
Oyibo 46, 46
Ozo title society 17, 30, 36
Painting 18
  body 15
Palm oil 6
Panels 27, 45
Pangolin 58
Pins 14
Planks 27
Platters 56
Portuguese 6, 49
Pots 20, *20*, 45
  musical 21
Pottery 20
  European 21
  figures 20-1, *20*
Raffia, weaving 12
Railway, Eastern 20
Rain Driver *58*, 61
Rattles 48
Real India 12
Ribbons 14
Rio Real 6, 13, 49, 50
Ritual specialist 5
Rivers state 5
Royal Niger Company 8
Rumuji town *10*, *33*, *54*, *57*
Sacks 12
Saws, crosscut 11, 27
Scarring: body 14
  face 14, 16, 17, 18, *38*, 49
  keloids *17*, 18, *41*, *51*
Sculpture 58
  cement 22
  Idoma 48
  mud *21*, 22
Shirt, dress 12
Shrines: household 37, *38*, 47
Ibudu 22

Skulls: human 39
  rams 39
Slaves and slave trade 6, 8, 50, 51
Societies 36
  Ekpe 36
  Human Leopard 35
  Ozo title 30, 36
  secret 35
Sombreiro river 49, 50, 53
Spears, throwing and ceremonial 11
Spirit 25, 33, 59
  animal 46, 56
  beautiful 16, 33
  familiar 38, *39*, 47, 53, 65
  fierce 34
  fish 56
  forest 35, 36
  goat 46
  nature 37, 47
  shrine 37
  tutelary *23*, *24*, 37
  water 35, 54, 56
Staffs 5, 26
  iron 26
Stars 28
Stilts 48, 55
Stools 26, 27, 28, *29*, 30
  Awka 30
  Ekpeya 30
  Ibibio 42
  Nupe 30
  Ozo Title 30
Style 8
  Cross River 8, 15, 18, *51*, *53*
  Ekoi 8
  geometric Ibo 28
  Ibibio 8, 42
  Ibo 8, 18, 62
  Ijo 8
  Isuama 56
Sudan, Central 12
Swords 11
Talbot, P. A. 44
Tools 11
Tortoise *33*, 34, 46, 58
Toys 40
Traveller *35*, 59
Triangles: curved 18, 48
  pointed 28
Tribal: marks 16, 47
  style 8
Trophy dance 41, 48
Troughs 26
Ubani tribe 49
Udi division 26
Ugbom *17*, 39, 41-3, *41*, *43*
  dance 39, 44
Ugwueke town 64
Ukara cloth 12
Ulaga 46
Uli, body painting *15*, 16
Umuahia town 49, 51
Urhobo (Edo) 5
War dance 39
Water spirits 34
Weapons 11
Weaving 12
Woodcarving 26
Yako tribe 66
Yam knife *42*
Yoruba 6, 12, 17, 24, 26, 27, 50, 58